British Life

ANNE COLLINS

Level 3

Series Editors: Andy Hopkins and Jocelyn Potter

Pearson Education Limited
Edinburgh Gate, Harlow,
Essex CM20 2JE, England
and Associated Companies throughout the world.

ISBN 0 582 435668

5 7 9 10 8 6

Design by Wendi Watson
Printed in China
SWTC/05

Published by Pearson Education Limited in association with Penguin Books Ltd,
both companies being subsidiaries of Pearson Plc

Photograph acknowledgements:
Rex Features: pp. 7 and 39;
Stockmarket: p. 9; David Watts: pp. 12-17 and 28-29;
Bruce Coleman/Jane Burton: p. 33
Mike Watson: pp. 26 and 32

For a complete list of titles available in the Penguin Readers series, please write to your local
Pearson Education office or to: Penguin Readers Marketing Department,
Pearson Education, Edinburgh Gate, Harlow, Essex CM20 2JE.

contents

Introduction

'Foreigners have ideas about what is 'British'.
But some of these things are not part of
most ordinary people's everyday lives.'

Most books about Britain give information for tourists. Visitors can learn about good hotels, nice restaurants, famous places and beautiful buildings. This book is about British life.

Who are the British? Are they the same as the English? And how is the UK different from Britain? Britain is not an easy nation to understand. To visitors, British life is sometimes very strange. Why, for example, do people talk about the weather so much?

Many things are changing in Britain, and one of them is family life. People's views on marriage and the family are very different from the views of their parents and grandparents. Business is also changing fast.

Another subject in this book is British food. Visitors to Britain don't always like British cooking. But why does British food have a bad name?

This book will tell you about ordinary British people. What do they like doing at weekends? What are their favourite television programmes? How important are sport and the National Lottery? What is the most popular pet? What is Crufts? What is a DIY centre? Read and find out!

Anne Collins was born in Yorkshire, England, but has lived in Edinburgh, Scotland, for the last six years. She has written a number of ELT readers, and she is interested in Scottish and English history. She likes everything about Scotland except the weather!

Map of the UK

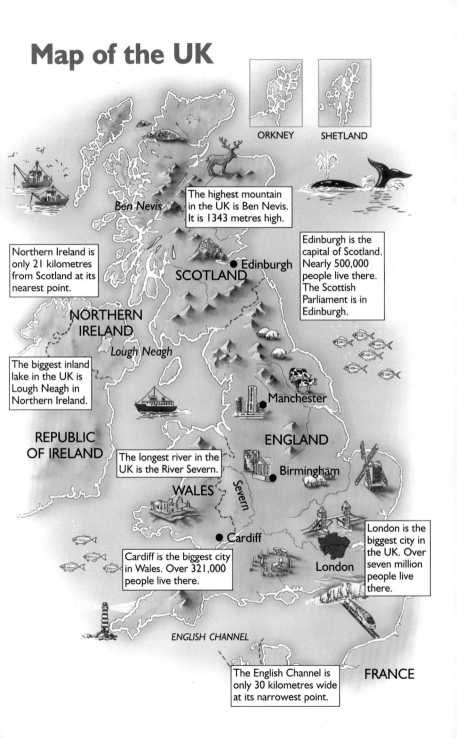

ORKNEY   SHETLAND

Ben Nevis

The highest mountain in the UK is Ben Nevis. It is 1343 metres high.

● Edinburgh

SCOTLAND

Edinburgh is the capital of Scotland. Nearly 500,000 people live there. The Scottish Parliament is in Edinburgh.

Northern Ireland is only 21 kilometres from Scotland at its nearest point.

NORTHERN IRELAND

Lough Neagh

The biggest inland lake in the UK is Lough Neagh in Northern Ireland.

REPUBLIC OF IRELAND

● Manchester

ENGLAND

The longest river in the UK is the River Severn.

Severn

● Birmingham

WALES

● Cardiff

Cardiff is the biggest city in Wales. Over 321,000 people live there.

London

London is the biggest city in the UK. Over seven million people live there.

ENGLISH CHANNEL

The English Channel is only 30 kilometres wide at its narrowest point.

FRANCE

The British

'When people say England, they sometimes mean Great Britain, sometimes the United Kingdom, sometimes the British Isles – but never England.'

George Mikes, *How to be an Alien*

Britain – the right names

Britain – or *Great Britain (GB)* – is the name for England, Wales and Scotland. Britain is the eighth largest island in the world. *The British Isles* is the name for England, Scotland, Wales, both parts of Ireland, the Isle of Man and the Channel Islands. *The United Kingdom (UK)* is England, Scotland, Wales and Northern Ireland. It is about 250,000 square kilometres in size and 1,000 kilometres from north to south. The British government is the government of the UK.

Many people think that 'English' is the same as 'British'. But England is only one of the four nations in the UK. The Scots, Welsh and Northern Irish are British too. They sometimes get angry when they are called 'English'.

There are also millions of British people whose parents first came to Britain in the 1950s and 1960s from the Caribbean, India, Pakistan, Hong Kong and other places. Their homes are mainly in the big English cities like London, Birmingham and Manchester.

Languages

Most British people speak English, but Gaelic is also spoken in the west and north of Scotland and in Northern Ireland. Welsh is spoken by over half a million people in Wales. The UK also has speakers of many other languages like Hindi, Urdu, Punjabi, Mandarin and Cantonese. There are a lot of different religions in Britain today too.

Some national differences

Dress

This picture shows some people's idea of a Scotsman. But when you see people in clothes like these in the streets of Edinburgh, they are probably not Scotsmen. They are probably American tourists! Scottish national dress is not worn by Scotsmen for everyday life, but only at special times, like weddings or dances.

Songs

The Scots, the Welsh and the Irish are very proud of their national songs. When the English play football against Scotland or Wales, the Scots sing *Flower of Scotland* and the Welsh sing *Land of My Fathers*. But the English national song is the same as the British national song – *God Save the Queen*.

Names

A person's name sometimes tells us where their family first came from. 'Mac' or 'Mc' in a surname (for example, McDonald) is always either Scottish or Irish. 'O'' in a surname (for example, O'Brien) is always Irish. Other surnames, like Morgan and Jones, are Welsh.

Sometimes, as a joke, Scotsmen are called 'Jock' or 'Jimmy' as a first name, Irishmen are called 'Paddy' or 'Mick' and Welshmen are called 'Dai' or 'Taffy'. But if you don't know someone well, don't call them by these names!

The British character

People say that Irish people talk a lot. They say that the Welsh are great singers. The Scots, they say, are not a very happy or fun-loving nation, and they are also very careful with money. Generally these descriptions are not true! But it *is* true that there are some very good Welsh actors and singers like Anthony Hopkins, Catherine Zeta Jones and Tom Jones.

Foreigners have ideas about what is 'British'. But some of these things are not part of most ordinary people's everyday life. The great British breakfast and afternoon tea, for example, are mostly found in hotels and 'bed and breakfast' places for tourists. And the British do not only drink tea these days. Coffee is popular too. They drink, on average, 3.39 cups of tea each day and 1.65 cups of coffee.

It takes time to know a British person well. British people are generally quite shy, and they do not make friends easily with strangers. Perhaps this is because they live on an island! And they are not good at learning foreign languages.

British people spend less money on clothes than the people of other European countries. Most of them are not very interested in clothes. Many British people wear suits to the office during the week, but at weekends they prefer to wear jeans.

British Conversation

Dr Johnson, a famous English writer, said over 200 years ago, 'When two Englishmen meet, their first talk is of the weather.' This is still true! Conversations between British people today often begin with the subject of the weather.

The Royal Family

How much do you know about the British royal family?

Answer these questions.

1 What is the family name of the present royal family?
   a Stuart **b** Windsor **c** Tudor

2 When did Queen Elizabeth II become Queen?
   a 1945 **b** 1952 **c** 1960

3 Who was her father?
   a George VI **b** Henry VIII **c** Prince Philip

4 What is the name of the Queen's younger sister?
   a Margaret **b** Anne **c** Mary

5 Which of these children of the Queen is NOT divorced?
   a Princess Anne **b** Prince Andrew **c** Prince Edward

6 Which of these places is NOT used as a royal home?
   a Buckingham Palace **b** Balmoral **c** the Houses of Parliament

7 What are the Queen's favourite animals?
   a birds **b** cats **c** dogs

8 Who was once part of the British team in the Olympic Games?
   a Prince Philip **b** Prince Charles **c** Princess Anne

9 How old was Princess Diana when she married?
   a 25 **b** 19 **c** 21

10 Which city did Princess Diana die in?
   a London **b** Paris **c** Rome

11 Who was Sarah Ferguson married to?
   a Prince Andrew **b** Prince Philip **c** Prince Charles

NOW TURN TO PAGE 40 FOR THE ANSWERS.

The royal family tree

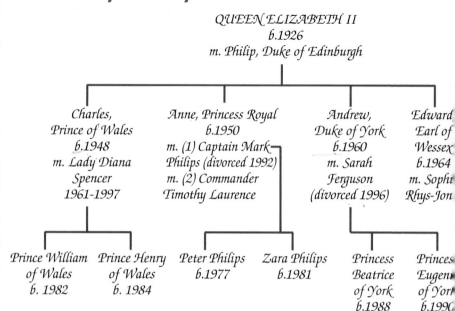

In the days of Queen Victoria (1837–1901), ordinary British people thought that the royal family was very special. Victoria, her husband and their nine children were seen as an example of perfect family life.

But today things are different. The Queen is still generally popular, but there have been too many problems with royal marriages. The Queen's sister and three of her four children – Charles, Anne and Andrew – are now divorced.

Prince Charles, the Queen's oldest son, married Princess Diana in 1981. Diana was young and beautiful and the newspapers and television were very interested in her. Soon she was more popular than Charles, her husband. But her marriage to Charles was not happy. When Diana died in a car accident in 1997 with her lover, Dodi Fayed, many British people were very sad.

The royal family is still very important for tourism in Britain. Special days like the State opening of Parliament in November and the royal weddings bring colour to people's lives. People in Britain enjoy reading about the lives of the royal family in newspapers and seeing them on television.

Britannia

Even the British royal family have to think about saving money sometimes. In the past few years, they have tried to find different ways of cutting costs.

The royal ship, the *Britannia*, was very famous for more than forty years. From 1953 to 1997 it travelled all over the world. It was used by the Queen and her family for business – for example, for visits by people in foreign governments – and for family holidays. After Prince Charles and Princess Diana were married, they had a holiday on the *Britannia*.

But many people thought that the royal family did not need an expensive ship like the *Britannia*. So finally the royal family stopped using it. It was taken to Edinburgh, and thousands of tourists visit it there. Today ordinary people can enjoy walking around this wonderful ship!

The British at Home

Owning a home

Today, most British people own the home that they live in. Of all the homes in Britain 67% (16.7 million homes) are owned by the people who live in them. In the south of England, the numbers are 74.7% in the south-east and 72.8% in the south-west. In Wales 71.5% of homes are owned by the people in them. In Northern Ireland the number is 71.4%. But in Scotland the number of home-owners has traditionally been lower (now 60.2% of homes).

Family size

On average, 2.4 people live as a family in one home in Britain. This number is smaller than in most other European countries. About 65% of people over the age of 65 live alone. When children grow up, they usually leave their parents' home for university or work. After they buy their own home, their parents do not usually come and live with them.

Number of people living in one house in Britain

	1961	1981	1998
One person	14%	22%	28%
Two people	29%	32%	35%
Three people	23%	17%	16%
Four people	18%	18%	14%
Five people	9%	7%	5%
Six or more people	7%	4%	2%

The Changing Family

The family in Britain is changing. By the year 2020 there will be fewer married people than single people.

In the past, people got married and stayed married. Divorce was very difficult and took a long time. The only reason for a short marriage was usually the death of the husband or wife. But today people's views on marriage are changing. Many couples, mostly in their twenties or thirties, live together without getting married. About 60% of these couples do get married in the end.

People get married at a later age now and many women do not want to have children immediately. They prefer to do well at their jobs first. So they often decide not to have a baby until they are in their late thirties, or even forties.

In the past, people married before they had children, but now about 40% of children in Britain are born to unmarried parents. The number of single-parent families in Britain is increasing. Single parents are usually divorced women (2/3) or women who have never married (1/3). The government gives help to single parents, but money can still be a problem. And studies show that, in general, children are happier and more successful in traditional two-parent families.

Divorce

The number of births in Britain is falling. There are fewer marriages, but more divorces. In 1969, the divorce laws were changed and divorce became quicker and easier. But can people walk away from marriages too easily now? Do couples not try hard enough to stay together?

The great divorce discussion

A popular British newspaper described Britain as 'the divorce capital of Europe'. There are 310,000 marriages a year, but 161,000 divorces. Why? A professional British woman in a top job wrote this surprising letter to the newspaper's Women's Page.

Why do so many people get divorced in Britain? The reason is very sad. British women are destroying their marriages!

In the past British women stayed at home, did the housework and had babies. When a husband came home from the office, his wife welcomed him. She looked nice, and dinner was ready. She asked him about his day and listened to all his problems. So husbands were happy with their wives and marriages were very successful.

But now British women want good jobs like their husbands, and they also want their husbands to help with the children and the housework.

If a husband has a bad day at work, his wife doesn't want to know about it. She wants to talk about her own day. She often gets angry because her husband doesn't help her more. In the end, the husband doesn't enjoy being at home. He leaves his wife for another woman, and the marriage ends in divorce.

The newspaper asked its readers for their views.

1 I agree with the letter. British women must do something about their marriages. When your husband comes home from work, cook his dinner. Ask him about his day. If he helps you, thank him. Don't tell him about your problems in the office or at home. Talk about things that are interesting to him. Then he'll want to come home to you.

2   This woman can't be serious! Women aren't destroying their marriages – men are! A working wife works hard all day. At night she's tired, too. But she has to cook, wash clothes and put the children to bed. And what does her selfish husband do? He sits down and watches TV!

3   A clever wife cooks her husband's meals, washes his shirts and makes his home life comfortable. Men want us to be like their mothers. What's wrong with that?

4   A wife isn't very interesting if she stays at home and does housework. Her husband will get bored and run away with his young secretary.

5   You don't like housework? Your husband doesn't like housework? Get a cleaner and save your marriage!

Stepfamilies

Children can suffer when their parents get divorced. When a divorced parent marries again, his or her children often find themselves living in a 'stepfamily' with a stepfather or stepmother. Do they call this new person 'Mum' or 'Dad'? Perhaps there are stepbrothers or stepsisters, too. It can be difficult for step-parents and their 'new' children, but it *can* work.

Now read the story. What do you think?

A Change of Heart

LUKE'S PARENTS ARE DIVORCED. LUKE LIVES WITH HIS MOTHER, BUT HE'S GOING TO SPEND THE WEEKEND WITH HIS FATHER.

Hurry up, Luke! Your father will be here soon.

Hey, there's a good film on TV tonight. Are you going to watch it?

No. Steve's taking me out to dinner.

Steve? Oh

Why doesn't Luke like Steve? Steve tries so hard to be friends with him.

Is Steve your boyfriend now?

Well – er – yes, he is. Don't you like him?

It's not that. But . . . he's not the same as Dad.

Your father and I are divorced now, Luke.

I miss my dad! I want us to be a family again.

Hello, Susan. Sorry I'm late.

That's OK. Luke's not ready. Come in and have a cup of coffee.

Thanks.

Hi, Dad. What are we doing today?

Lunch at McDonald's first. Then I've got tickets for the big game.

Alan's still a good father to Luke.

Bye, Mum. See you tomorrow!

Bye, Luke!

I want her to come with us.

LATER THAT AFTERNOON.

You're very quiet, Luke. Didn't you enjoy the game?

Oh, yes. But I was thinking about you and Mum. Why did you get divorced?

13

15

16

But I'm Luke's father.

When you left me, it was the end of the world for me. But now I've got a good job and a man who loves me. I don't need you, Alan.

Yes, and you're a wonderful father. Luke loves you and I want you to see him. Goodbye, Alan.

It's too late for you and Dad to be together, isn't it?

I'm sorry, Luke. Please try to understand.

Luke, I want to be with Steve. But I know you need to accept him. Luke?... Luke?

17

Faces of Business

Britain still produces many things in its factories. But today British people have more money to spend. They want to enjoy themselves. So the fastest growing businesses in the UK are service industries – hotels, restaurants, travel, shopping, and computer and financial services. About 75% of British jobs are in service industries; they employ over twenty million people.

Many British companies have added new services to increase their business. Large supermarkets like Sainsbury's and Tesco do not only sell food. They also sell TVs and videos, clothes and petrol. They even offer financial services. Most supermarkets open seven days a week, and many other shops are also open on Sundays now.

A 'round-the-clock' service

The usual working day in Britain starts at 9 a.m. and finishes at 5 p.m. Most people work a five-day week. But now many companies want to give their customers a 'round-the-clock' service 24 hours a day, 365 days a year.

Banks did this first. Many people needed money outside the banks' opening hours. So the banks started 'hole-in-the-wall' machines. With a plastic bank card and a personal number, customers could get money out at any time, even in the middle of the night.

How hard do British people work?

The British working week is, on average, the longest of any country in Europe. In 1998 a new law was made. Workers do not have to work more than an average of 48 hours a week if they don't want to. But about 22% of British workers do work more than a 48-hour week. Men work longer hours than women. British employers must give their workers four weeks paid holiday every year.

Full-time and part-time work

About 45% of British workers are women, but many of them are in part-time jobs. About 44% of women work part-time. Many women do not want a full-time job because they want to spend time with their family. But only 9% of men work part time, usually because they cannot find a full-time job. About 16% of men and 7% of women are self-employed. They do not work for a company, but for themselves.

British businesses

There are about 3.7 million businesses in the UK. Many of these are large companies. About 3,000 British businesses employ more than 500 people. Of the top 500 European companies, about 150 are British.

Average hours usually worked per week by full-time employees, 1998	Hours	
	Men	Women
United Kingdom	45.7	40.7
Portugal	42.1	39.6
Greece	41.7	39.3
Spain	41.2	39.6
Germany	40.4	39.3
Luxembourg	40.3	37.4
France	40.3	38.7
Austria	40.2	39.8
Sweden	40.2	40.0
Finland	40.1	38.2
Italy	39.7	36.3
Denmark	39.3	37.7
Netherlands	39.2	38.5
Belgium	39.1	37.5
EU average	41.3	39.0

Call centres

Many big companies use 'call centres'. In these centres, people speak to customers who often telephone outside the usual working hours. They take orders and answer questions. They also make calls to customers at home to increase the company's business.

THE CALL CENTRE

IT WAS MY FIRST DAY WORKING IN A CALL CENTRE. I WAS FEELING VERY NERVOUS.

I've never seen so many computers and telephones in my life. I hope I'm going to like it here.

BUT THEN THINGS GOT INTERESTING.

Hi, I'm Jim. Welcome to the phone farm!

Oh, hi, I'm Emma. What do you mean, 'phone farm'?

You'll soon find out.

A FEW MINUTES LATER.

There's a list of customers' phone numbers on your computer. You call them and tell them about the company's new services.

Hello, Emma. I'm Marian. I'm going to show you how to make calls. You'll start calling customers this afternoon.

But how do I know what to say?

But ... I need more time to learn.

It's all here, on this piece of paper.

21

The City of London

The City of London is the biggest financial centre in Europe, and one of the world's main financial centres – the other two are Tokyo and New York. The City's international activities are very important and the UK is the world's largest single market for international banking. Banks from about eighty countries have offices in London.

The world of international banking is very exciting. Charles Rogers works in the London offices of a Dutch bank. He often travels to Europe and other countries for his job.

What's the history of the City of London?

The Romans built a city, Londinium, in AD 50*. It was about a square mile in size and it had a wall all round it.

In the 1300s, money-lenders from Lombardy, in Italy, came to Londinium – or London, as it was now called. They started doing business in the area of the walled city. There's still a Lombard Street in the City today. There's no wall now, but the area's still called the City of London and it's the most important business centre in Britain. It's still sometimes called 'the square mile', and it has hundreds of banks, insurance companies and financial centres. The Bank of England is in the City.

*AD: after the birth of Jesus Christ

What are the main kinds of business in the City?

Banking and insurance. Banks were places where people kept their money. Insurance companies started because Britain had a lot of shipowners. Their ships sailed all over the world, doing business with foreign countries. When a ship got lost at sea, shipowners lost everything. So they paid money to insurance companies to protect themselves.

Why is the City of London the financial centre of Europe?

There are a number of reasons, but London's the capital of England, and English is the international language of business.

Do you enjoy working in the City?

Yes, very much. It's a very busy and exciting place. Nearly a million people work here during the day – that's more than the population of Frankfurt. But the City is only busy during the day. At night it's very quiet. Fewer than 8,000 people live there.

How many banks are there in the City?

About six hundred.

Who's 'The Old Lady of Threadneedle Street'?

This is another name for the Bank of England. This is the central bank of Britain. It also prints British banknotes. The Bank's main offices are in Threadneedle Street, in the City.

The British and Food

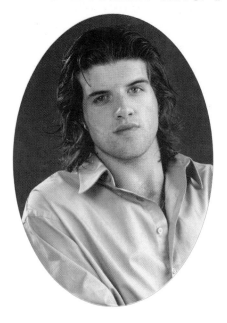

Paul White works as a cook in a top London hotel. What does he think about the British and Food?

'Visitors to Britain generally agree about one thing – British cooking. "It's terrible!" they say. "You can cook vegetables in so many interesting ways. But the British cook vegetables for too long, so they lose their taste." These visitors eat in the wrong places. The best British cooking is in good restaurants and hotels, or at home.

'British tastes have changed a lot over the past twenty years. In 1988 the national average for each person was 352 grams of "red" meat each week, but now it's less than 250 grams. People prefer chicken and fresh fish. And more people are interested in healthy eating these days. In 1988 the national average was 905 grams of fruit and fruit juices each week, but now it's nearly 2,000 grams.

'The British have a "sweet tooth". They love cakes, chocolates and sweets. At my hotel we cook traditional British puddings and our customers love them. Can you imagine a pudding made mostly with bread and butter? It exists in British cooking – "Bread and Butter Pudding". It's great!'

Changing tastes

Today many people want food to be quick and easy. When both parents are working, they cannot cook large meals in the evenings. 'Ready-made' meals from supermarkets and Marks and Spencer and 'take-away' meals from fast food restaurants are very popular. If you are feeling tired or lazy, you can even phone a local restaurant. They will bring the food to your house.

Eating out

Twenty years ago, British people usually ate at home. They only went out for a meal at special times, like for somebody's birthday. But today, many people eat out at least once a week.

In the past, traditional steakhouses were very popular places, but now many people prefer foreign food. Every British town has Indian and Chinese restaurants, and large towns have restaurants from many other countries too.

Pubs are also very popular. There are over 60,000 pubs in the UK (53,200 in England and Wales, 5,200 in Scotland and 1,600 in Northern Ireland). British people drink an average of 99.4 litres of beer every year. More than 80% of this beer is drunk in pubs and clubs.

Scones

Scones are a popular and traditional part of British afternoon tea. They are eaten with a cup of tea or coffee. They are easy and fun to make.

For 9 – 10 scones, you will need:
200 grams flour
1/2 teaspoon salt
50 grams butter
1/2 cup milk

1   Put the flour and salt into a bowl. Work the small pieces of butter into the flour and salt with your fingers.

2   Add the milk quickly and mix with a knife.

3 Take out of the bowl and make into a large flat shape on a table.

4 Cut into 9 or 10 round shapes. Put a little milk on the top of each.

5 Cook in a hot oven (200°c, Gas 6) for 7 – 10 minutes until golden-brown.

6 Put the scones on a plate and offer them to your guests. Eat them with butter. Enjoy!

The British and tea

The British population (over the age of ten) drinks about 200,000,000 cups of tea a day. That is an average of nearly 1,040 cups of tea a year for each person. Tea – mostly green tea from China – came to Britain in the late 1500s, but it was only for the very rich. It became cheaper about three hundred years later, when it was planted in India and later in Ceylon (Sri Lanka). People from all classes started drinking it. But some people thought that too much tea was bad for your health. So they started putting milk in it, to make it healthier!

Afternoon tea, high tea, lunch and dinner

Afternoon tea is a small meal, not a drink. Now most ordinary British families do not have time for afternoon tea at home, but in the past it was a tradition. It became popular about a hundred and fifty years ago, when rich ladies invited their friends to their houses for an afternoon cup of tea. They started offering their visitors sandwiches and cakes too. Soon everybody was enjoying this exciting new meal.

But the British working population did not have afternoon tea. They had a meal at about midday, and a meal after work, between five and seven o'clock. This meal was called 'high tea', or just 'tea'. Some families in Scotland and the north of England still have 'high tea' and some restaurants in these areas offer it too. High tea is a big meal with a main dish – meat or fish – followed by bread and butter and cakes. You drink lots of cups of tea with high tea.

Today most people have a meal between 12 and 2 p.m. In the past, this meal was called 'dinner' in working families. But now most people call it 'lunch'. 'Dinner' has become a bigger meal in the evenings.

Weekend Activities

What do British people like doing at weekends?

TV programmes

You can learn a lot about British life from TV magazines. Notice how many programmes are about wildlife, pets and holidays. A lot of other programmes are about cooking, gardening and things for the home. There are programmes about moving house. There is even a programme about housework!

8.00 Changing Rooms
CHOICE
Two days of high drama are in
a plaster disaster with her bi
Anna Ryder Richardson trans
lounge into a stylish living room for artis
south east London. Presented by Carol S

8.30 DIY S ...h Walker. Executive ...
In the last programme of the curr
come to the rescue of firefighters
tried to turn their old recreation ro
hall using a fire axe. With Lowri Tu
Series producer Mark Bristow; Executive pro
9.00 BBC News

3.30 Gardeners' World With Alan Titchmarsh. Ga
Search explores the garden of actress Carol Boyd
(Linda Snell from Radio 4's *The Archers*). (W)(T)(R) ...
4.00 Yes Minister Open Government: lim ...

8.00 Ground Force
CHOICE
Alan Titchmarsh, Charlie Dimmock
travel to Alloa near Stirling where th
small garden accessible by raising
year on, Charlie and Tommy return
up on the garden's progress – onl
couple more jobs to be done. **See**

DIY* and garden centres

Many people in Britain are very proud of their houses and gardens. They want their homes and gardens to look nice. Every British town has one or more DIY centres, like B & Q, and garden centres. They are like supermarkets for the home and garden. These places are very popular with British home-owners at weekends.

DIY centres sell things like wood for making shelves. Garden centres sell plants for the garden and things for the home too. People enjoy doing work on their home and garden. It is cheaper than employing a builder or gardener. But money is not the only reason why DIY and garden centres are so popular. You can get very good ideas there too. And DIY and gardening are fun!

* DIY: Do-It-Yourself

A Nation of Animal Lovers

'If you go for a walk with a friend, don't say a word for hours; if you go out for a walk with your dog, keep chatting to him.'

George Mikes, *How to be an Alien*

The British are traditionally a nation of animal lovers. This is clear from the large number of animal programmes on TV. There are programmes about wildlife in Britain and other countries, and about pets at home. There are programmes like *Animal Hospital* about sick animals and the working lives of animal doctors. Some programmes try to find new homes for unwanted or homeless animals. All these programmes are very popular.

There is a pet in nearly 50% of the 24.2 million homes in Britain.

The Most Popular Pets in Britain

Fish	26.6 million
Cat	7.7 million
Dog	6.7 million
Rabbit	1.5 million
Budgerigar	1.0 million
Hamster	1.0 million
Guinea pig	0.8 million

Budgerigar   Guinea Pig

Rabbit   Hamster

Battersea Dogs' Home

Battersea Dogs' Home in London is a very famous home for unwanted dogs and cats. It was started in 1860 by Mrs Mary Tealby, because she was worried about all the homeless animals on the streets of London. The home has taken in 2,734,386 dogs. Since 1883, it has taken in cats too. In 1999, nearly 14,000 dogs and cats came to the home. By the end of the year, homes were found for 65% of these. The home even has its own magazine, *Paws*.

Crufts Dog Show

Crufts is a very popular dog show that takes place in Britain every March. It was started by Charles Cruft in 1891 as a way of selling a kind of dog food! For many years it was held in London, but in 1991 it moved to Birmingham. This year 25,000 dogs are taking part in Crufts. Over 100,000 people visit Crufts each year.

It Can Only Happen in Britain!

The rat at platform one has just made your train late!

The Echo January 13 2000

An SSPCA* officer was called to Stirling station today because passengers were worried about a large white rat on the line. Three trains passed over it, but the rat was unhurt. The Scottish railway company, Scotrail, closed the line. Then passengers watched as the officer carefully caught the rat. It bit him, but he took it away safely.

An officer from Scotrail said, 'We try to protect all wild animals and pets. At first the rat was very frightened, but now he's fine.

'We've called him Ronnie. He needs a a good home. People think rats are dirty. But they make great pets!'

*SSPCA: a group that helps animals

The National Lottery

Every Saturday and Wednesday evening, people all over Britain excitedly turn on their TVs. Are six numbers going to change their lives? Have they won the National Lottery?

The National Lottery was only started in 1994, but it has quickly become an important part of ordinary British life. Over 70% of British homes now take part in the Saturday night lottery. In 1998–99 they spent an average of £3.80 every week on lottery tickets. Each ticket costs £1.

The British National Lottery is the biggest in the world. A new game, Thunderball, was started in 1999. The winning amounts on Thunderball are not as large, but there is a greater possibility of winning.

Most of us dream of winning millions of pounds. This is the answer to all our problems! We can begin a wonderful new life and never worry about money again. But then we read newspaper stories about unhappy Lottery winners. How can this be? Did they spend all their money too quickly on fast cars and expensive houses? Or did their friends change towards them when they became rich?

Perhaps the winnings are too large. But 28p out of every £1 of the ticket money is spent on things that help Britain, perhaps in the arts, sport or health. So when people lose, they are still helping to make Britain a better place.

Some unusual winners

British newspapers like printing stories about people who have won the Lottery. These stories are usually very interesting.

IS IT EVER TOO LATE TO WIN THE LOTTERY?

A GROUP OF FIVE OLD PEOPLE IN A NURSING home won over five million pounds on the National Lottery last Saturday night – over a million pounds each. The oldest person in the group is 87 and the youngest is 77.

Most Lottery winners want to change their lives immediately. But these five old friends want to change their lives as little as possible. They don't want to leave the nursing home, or even go on holiday. 'We have no reason to leave,' they said. 'This is our home and we're very happy here. We have good food, TV, friends – everything that we want.'

What exciting things are they going to buy with their money? 'Well, perhaps an electric chair on wheels,' said one. Is that all? No new houses or fast cars? 'But what can we do with Ferraris at our age?' replied the old people. 'Cars are no use to us. We need help just to move around the home!'

Professional financial people are sent to visit Lottery winners by the company which runs the National Lottery. They help winners decide how to spend their money. But these five old people won't have any problems. They don't want big changes in their lives. They just want things to stay as they are.

THE BRITISH
and SPORT

'A game like cricket... goes on for three
days and never seems to start...'

Bill Bryson, Notes from a Small Island

How much do you know about sport in Britain?
Answer these questions.

1 Which sport do British people most enjoy watching on TV?
   a cricket **b** football **c** swimming

2 Which sport do British people most enjoy doing?
   a running **b** swimming **c** walking

3 What sport is played at Wimbledon?
   a tennis **b** football **c** cricket

4 What sport is played at Lord's in North London?
   a football **b** cricket **c** tennis

5 At what time of year does Wimbledon take place?
   a Christmas **b** autumn **c** summer

6 Where is Wembley?
   a London **b** Scotland **c** Wales

7 How many people are there in a cricket team?
   a ten **b** eleven **c** eight

8 What kind of animals run in the Grand National?
   a dogs **b** horses **c** none

9 Which universities are in the Boat Race?
   a London and Oxford **b** Edinburgh and London
   c Oxford and Cambridge

10 Where did the 2002 Commonwealth Games take place?
   a London **b** Manchester **c** Edinburgh

NOW TURN TO PAGE 41
FOR THE ANSWERS.

THE BRITISH
on Holiday

In the late 1800s, rich people in Britain started going on holiday. By the beginning of the 1900s, the British working population were taking holidays too. Traditionally, families spent their holidays by the sea. Many seaside towns still have streets full of hotels and 'bed and breakfast' places for summer visitors.

The most popular holiday areas in Britain are the West Country (Devon and Cornwall), the south of England and Scotland. In the last twenty years, the number of British people on traditional seaside holidays has fallen by 20%. But one place in Britain is still very popular – Blackpool, on the north-west coast of England. In 1998, 7.1 million people visited Blackpool beach. The lights at night are very famous. People travel a long way to see them.

Holidays abroad

In 1998, for the first time, more British people had holidays abroad than in Britain. Twenty-nine million holidays were taken abroad and 27 million holidays were taken in Britain. Most British tourists buy 'package holidays' when they travel to other countries. The cost is for travel and a place to stay.

Europe is still more popular for British holiday-makers than other parts of the world. More people go on holidays to Spain than to any other country. But the USA is popular too. As air travel becomes cheaper, people are starting to go to the Caribbean countries and Australia for their holidays.

Britons abroad: the most popular holiday places

Spain	France	USA	Greece	Italy
27.5%	20.2%	7.0%	5.3%	4.0%

Evenings Out

The theatre

There are 300 professional theatres in Britain. Some are owned privately, but most are not. Every large town in Britain has at least one theatre. London has about a hundred. Famous London theatres are the Royal National Theatre, the Barbican Centre and the Royal Court Theatre. The average number of people at each play in 1998 was 744.

There are some excellent British actors, like Derek Jacobi and Peter O'Toole, and actresses, like Helen Mirren and Diana Rigg. Tom Stoppard is a very good modern writer of plays. Shakespeare's plays are still very popular. Many British plays move successfully to other countries. But the world's longest running play of any kind is Agatha Christie's murder mystery, *The Mousetrap*. This play, at St Martin's Theatre, London, is now in its forty-eighth year.

Cinema

Cinema is very popular in Britain. There are about 125 million cinema visits each year. Visitors paid more money to see *Titanic* than any other film. In one year it made £69 million in Britain.

The British are good at making amusing films. *The Full Monty* (1997) and *Four Weddings and a Funeral* (1994) were made by British companies and are the highest earning British films of all time. *The Full Monty* cost £1.6 million to make. It earned £161 million around the world. *Four Weddings* cost £2 million to make. It earned £155 million. The third highest earning British film is *Bean: The Ultimate Disaster Movie* (1997) with Rowan Atkinson. This film made £146 million.

American film companies often make films in Britain. For example, *Shakespeare in Love* (Best Picture, 1999) was produced by an American company, but was made in Britain. It used mostly British actors and actresses like Ralph Fiennes and Judi Dench.

Musicals

The most famous British writer of musicals (musical plays) is Andrew Lloyd Webber. He has his own company, The Really Useful Group Ltd. Some of his musicals are *Jesus Christ Superstar* (1972), *Evita* (1976), *Cats* (1981), *Starlight Express* (1986) and *The Phantom of the Opera* (1986).

The Phantom of the Opera

These have all been very popular and successful. *Cats* has played in 250 cities around the world. *Jesus Christ Superstar* has played in 15 countries. But the most successful musical is *The Phantom of the Opera*. Since it opened, over 52 million people have seen it.

ANSWERS

Answers to questions on the British royal family (p. 5)

Give yourself 3 points for each correct answer.

1 **b** Windsor. The Stuarts and the Tudors are the names of past British royal families.
2 **b** 1952, after her father died.
3 **a** George VI. Henry VIII was king from 1509 to 1547. Prince Philip is the Queen's husband.
4 **a** Margaret. She was born in 1930 and is four years younger than the Queen.
5 **c** Prince Edward. He married Sophie Rhys-Jones on 19 June, 1999. Their titles are the Earl of Wessex and the Countess of Wessex.
6 **c** The Houses of Parliament. Buckingham Palace is the royal family's famous London home. They use Balmoral, in Scotland, as a holiday home.
7 **c** Dogs. The Queen has eight small pet dogs.
8 **c** Princess Anne. She was part of the British horse-riding team in the 1976 Olympics in Montreal.
9 **b** 19. Charles and Diana married on 29 July, 1981.
10 **b** Paris. Diana was killed in a car accident on 31 August, 1997.
11 **a** Prince Andrew. Andrew and Sarah divorced in 1996. They have two daughters, Princess Beatrice and Princess Eugenie.

27–33 points You are clearly very interested in the British royal family. Perhaps you can write a book about them!
15–24 points You know something about the British royal family. But you still have a lot to learn.
0–12 points Don't you know anything about the British royal family? You should read more magazines!

Answers to questions on the British and Sport (p. 36)

Give yourself 3 points for each correct answer.

1 **b** Football. In 1998, 23.7 million people in the UK watched the World Cup game between England and Argentina.

2 **c** Walking. This is popular with men and women. It means all kinds of walking – for example, long walks in the country, or difficult hill-walking.

3 **a** Tennis. A tennis club was started at Wimbledon in 1868. Today's top tennis players all want to win at Wimbledon. In 1999 over 457,000 people went to watch tennis there. The two top British players, Tim Henman and Greg Rusedski, are in the world's top ten players.

4 **b** Cricket. The 1999 World Cricket Cup was played at Lord's, and twelve countries took part. Around 476,800 people watched the games. Australia won the Cup.

5 **c** Summer – two weeks every June.

6 **a** London. (North London)

7 **b** Eleven.

8 **b** Horses. The Grand National takes place every April at Aintree near Liverpool. Over 300 million people around the world watch the race each year.

9 **c** Oxford and Cambridge. The Boat Race takes place every April on the River Thames in London.

10 **b** Manchester.

24–30 points Excellent! You probably know more than some British people about British sport.

12–21 points You know a little about British sport. Read more about it!

0–9 points You really aren't very interested in British sport, are you?

ACTIVITIES

Pages 1–8

Before you read

1 Name these places in your own country.
   a the longest river
   b the highest mountain
   c the biggest lake
   d the most important cities

2 Find these words in your dictionary. They are all in the book.
   Put forms of the words in the sentences below.
   average   character   divorce   isle   royal   tradition
   a The Opening of Parliament is a ....
   b What is the ..... population of the smaller British ..... ?
   c She didn't have the right ..... for marriage – and now
   she's ....

After you read

3 Are these sentences right or wrong?
   a The British are all English.
   b O'Brien is a Scottish name.
   c British people have afternoon tea every day.
   d All the Queen's children are divorced.
   e The royal family don't use the *Britannia* now.
   f About 30% of British people own their homes.

4 Answer these questions.
   a How many nations are there in the UK?
   b Where is Gaelic spoken?
   c How did Princess Diana die?
   d Where is the *Britannia* today?
   e Which of the nations in the UK has the smallest number of
   home-owners?
   f How many people are there in an average British family, living
   in one house?

Pages 9–25

Before you read

5 Is family life changing in your country? Is it getting better or worse?

6 Find these words in your dictionary.

couple   financial   increase   insurance   service industry step-family

a Which are words for people?

b Which words are about business?

c Which word means get bigger?

After you read

7 Answer these questions about *A Change of Heart.*

a Why doesn't Luke like Steve?

b What do you think Luke will do now?

c What will Susan do?

8 Work with a friend. Have this conversation from *The Call Centre.*

Student A: You are Emma. Telephone Mrs Brown and tell her about East-West's shopping services. Ask if she is interested.

Student B: You are Mrs Brown. Ask and answer questions.

Pages 26–39

Before you read

9 Discuss these questions.

a What kind of food is famous in your country?

b What do people in your country like doing at weekends?

10 Find these words in your dictionary.

chat   cricket   flour   lottery   nursing-home   pudding rat   scone

Find the words for:

a food   **c** a sport

b an animal   **d** a building

What does *chat* mean?

After you read

11 Find pairs of words that go together..

scones   film   *The Mousetrap*   pudding   Crufts   play
beer   afternoon tea   dog show   pubs   *The Full Monty*
bread and butter

12 Finish these sentences.

a Some families in Scotland	own a pet.
b The most popular pets in Britain	for British holiday-makers.
c Nearly half of British homes	started in 1994.
d The National Lottery	are cats.
e Spain is more popular than France	have 'high tea'.

Writing

13 Write a letter to the newspaper about 'the great divorce discussion'. What do you think?

14 You are Emma in *The Call Centre*. Tell Marian that you cannot continue to work in the call centre. Explain why. Write your conversation.

15 Choose one of your favourite foods. Tell a friend how to make it.

16 What are the most interesting things about Britain and British people? Give your opinions.

Answers for the Activities in this book are available from your local office or alternatively write to:
Penguin Readers Marketing Department, Pearson Education, Edinburgh Gate, Harlow, Essex
CM20 2JE.